PISCES

HOROSCOPE

2019

Pisces Horoscope

2019

Copyright © 2018 by Crystal Sky

www.ohoroscope.com

3

Acknowledgment:

I would like to express my gratitude to my family, who nurture and support my dreams.

Pisces Horoscope

2019

January Horoscope

ASTROLOGICAL & ZODIAC ENERGY

EXPANSIVE~ PROGRESSIVE ~ MOTIVATED

WORK & CAREER

You are headed successfully towards the achievement of a significant goal you have been working towards this year. As you see the glittering path ahead, you are inspired to continue to develop this potential. It is a journey which holds every promise dear to your heart, you shine brightly and realize incredible fulfillment by committing yourself fully to this venture. You embark on an enchanting journey which attracts positive energy around your awareness, you develop skills which are finely tuned, and enable you to practice your talents in versatile and innovative ways. You are busy making plans this January, your schedule is tight because you are hoping to develop a significant path towards the realization of your dreams. Long-term goals are slowly becoming a reality, and this is expanding your awareness into what may be next on your way.

Your spirit is restless, and you think of ways to draw more interest in your life. You seek a deeper more profound bond with another, and as you envision the future, you hope to develop a more emotionally connected future. This is a time of emerging self-awareness, which reveals hidden aspects of your spirit which desire to be expressed. You think of setting forth on a journey which embodies your dreams, hopes, and aspirations. You are ready to embark on a fresh phase of development, and by taking stock of where you hope to go, you set forth carefully, knowing you have done the careful considerations needed to succeed on this journey. This January your emotions are bewitching you to expand your horizons, and embrace your personal vision. This is taking you to a time which sees you express your needs authentically and emotionally to others in your life.

IDEAS & CREATIVITY

Your need for stability, security, and tradition may be at odds with the restless and unsettled energy which envelopes you this month. You are being guided to gain insight into the way forward by weighing your options and making a decision based on your own inner intuition. As you navigate the path ahead, you develop the necessary self-confidence to become a force to be reckoned with. The search for excellence and ecstatic experiences marks your passage, and you find yourself seeking out like-minded people. You cultivate a broader tribe of diverse people to engage with in lively conversation. You are marked by a significant sensitivity which allows you to be blessed with a real sense of what's next on the horizon if you take the time to look within and contemplate where you are guided towards. When you do this your energies are so directed that you find life much smoother.

ISSUES & HURDLES

You may be feeling doubt and anxiety during the first half of January. You find yourself caught up in the midst of pursuing a goal you have wanted to achieve, but there may be some doubt and frustration regarding developing this idea. This prospect does have many ups and downs, and it takes you on a winding path of progression, it does test your strength and force you to deal with the complicated feelings that limit your progress. Transformation is empowering, but you do need to put things in the correct perspective so you can recognize the importance of dealing with fear and understand that you are able to work around the hurdles which create barriers against your progress. During the January 21st Super-Moon, you uncover your inner feelings and find your rhythm which enables you to develop creative and innovative solutions to hurdles which have held your progress back, this sees confusion dissolve, and it's full steam ahead next month

February Horoscope

PERSISTENT ~ TENACIOUS ~ UNDAUNTED

WORK & CAREER

The beginning of February, you are able to plot a course forward, no longer bound to restrictions which hindered your progress last month, you embrace a sense of liberation into your life which sees your spirit free to soar. The positive elements of this months see you confronting challenges head-on as you use your influence to find solutions which continue to draw stability into your world. You are money-wise, influential, and shrewd. This is a month which symbolizes the gaining of knowledge and brings vitality and good fortune into your surroundings. It sees you deeply involved as you persevere with challenge orientated goals until you see real success. This inspires and captivates your imagination, and leads to you towards broadening your horizons in diverse ways. There are many steps

11

*to the achievement of goals, and you plot a course
forward efficiently.*

LOVE & ROMANCE

*Your energy is seated in the realm of emotions this
February. You enter a path which takes you towards
emotional fulfillment. You are motivated, inspired,
and in tune with your inner feelings. Romantic and
idealistic, this is a time which sees your heart rule.
Your emotional awareness expresses your deepest
feelings, and you create a firm foundation for
moving well-being in your life. You express energy
which is creative, passionate, and sensitive. Your life
is improving, your enthusiasm is reawakened, and
you appreciate the emotional abundance which flows
into your surroundings. Your intuition works
beautifully in tandem with your emotional
awareness to guide you towards expanding your
horizons into new areas of potential. This sees your
life blossom, and you experience a wonderful sense of
harmony and happiness in your life. It does suggest
romance is at the forefront of this seductive energy,
and couples can expect an emotionally fulfilling ever
on the 14th of February to highlight how meaningful*

your personal life is. For singles, this is a month of expanding your awareness and horizons, as you take steps to diverge from your usual patterns and shake things up a bit.

IDEAS & CREATIVITY

You overflow with abundance, the reward is assured and likely to soon flow into your life. You can reach for your dreams as what you seek is likely to be fulfilled, bringing you unexpected opportunities, blessings, and positive results. Advancement is expected this February, and as you progress towards the realization of goals, you overcome obstacles and resonate power. Your character is imaginative, free-spirited, and disciplined. You work diligently and embrace the changes which flow into your surroundings. Positive signs arrive and leave your feeling empowered, capable, and able to expand your horizons. This is a time of radiant and dynamic potential, allowing you to glimpse the infinite possibilities that are available in your life. You appreciate the abundance which arrives, as your hard work has paid off and enabled you to enjoy some well-earned luxury. The Super-Moon in Leo on

13

February 19th takes you on a creative journey which sees fresh ideas flow into your mind, this sets the stage for an enticing vision which you will likely put in motion soon.

ISSUES & HURDLES

You may find yourself clashing with others as you can push emotional buttons with your words. Your communication is marked by a curiosity that can feel intrusive to sensitive people. You may be faced with coming to terms with a sense of rejection, and need to control your tendency towards excesses of all kinds. The challenge of this situation is in recognizing how your insecurity interferes with your real potential. As you attune yourself to the vibrations of others, you may find this compounds the difficulties that surround you. You may discover separating from the situation enables your balance to be restored, and helps draw a sense of harmony back into your surroundings. Don't be brought into the drama, focus on your own goals, as this will enable you to navigate through a turbulent time efficiently.

March Horoscope

ASTROLOGICAL THEME & ZODIAC ENERGY

CONSTRUCTIVE ~ THOUGHTFUL ~ VISIONARY

WORK & CAREER

All career goals are attainable, you overcome limitations and seek material rewards. This is a creative time which captures your imagination, enabling you to focus your energy on developing your goals. You are disciplined and work diligently to achieve stability and material success. You feel encouraged by a succession of positive signs that your finances are improving, this inspires you to persist and keep reaching for your dreams. The conditions are right for you to thrive, you have what it takes to accomplish goals, and you draw abundance into your world. As you overflow with gifts, you are able to share your knowledge with others, who also benefit by being around you. You may even be presented with a significant opportunity for growth and can relax and enjoy a time of heightened stability, growth, and security in your life. Tangible results are approaching.

LOVE & ROMANCE

March is a month of developing your emotional realm. You arrive at a path of nurturing your sensitive side. You are guided towards strengthening your heart, intuition, and emotions. You come alive as your feelings blossom, and your heart feels the stirrings of desire and emotional abundance. This takes you on a journey which opens your heart and enlivens your emotions to fully explore your feelings and sensitive side. You move in alignment with your passion, this is just the beginning, the more authentic you are with yourself, the more you can celebrate a more harmonious and connected future. This month signifies celebrations and the coming together of valued friends to celebrate a situation in your life. Positive energy flows around you, and you find you have much to feel happy about as you develop your presence on emotional levels.

IDEAS & CREATIVITY

You are blessed with tremendous diligence and dedication, and this has you realize the lovely potential available in your life. You have many passions and are adept at developing your goals. The perseverance you employ towards achieving a high result pays you dividends this March. This is a time of utilizing the powers of your mind, and this will likely connect you with some form of innovation in the world of ideas and theories which helps you explore the world around you by studying its lessons first hand. You have a creative ability which enables you to make a unique mark on the planet. Your personal appeal combined with your natural talents which lets you a high level of success. As you carefully follow your vision, you are likely to give form to your unique ideas, which take you on a journey of expansion and adventure.

ISSUES & HURDLES

Life is likely to be demanding. Stresses and strains arrive, and you are met with opposition. Trying different approaches may help you deal with the difficulties which enter your surroundings mid-March. Valuable lessons about diplomacy and flexibility are able to be learned. This may be a painful time, but you can use it as a catalyst for personal growth. Liberate and free yourself from the oppressive energy of others who seek to impose their fixed viewpoints on your life. Arguments and disagreements are indicated, but you can stand up for yourself and do battle against the war of words which may enter your surroundings. You may just need to walk away and not be drawn into the drama. Whatever the case knowing what is ahead will give you the inside knowledge needed, so it doesn't come as a big surprise when it arrives.

April Horoscope

ASTROLOGICAL THEME & ZODIAC ENERGY

TASTEFUL ~ IMAGINATIVE ~ ORGANIZED

WORK & CAREER

Your high idealism and good practical instincts are a formidable combination as you seek to develop a particular goal in your life this April. You are blessed with a unique ability and talent to turn your visions into concrete reality, and you are likely to make significant progress soon and enjoy substantial benefits to your working life. There is very little which will hold you back from overcoming the obstacles which have been hindering your progress recently. As you accomplish what you set out to achieve, you find a sense of happiness and liberation is reclaimed in your life. Your emphasis is on developing your career path, and you are blessed with high energy and an incredible capacity for hard work which helps you realize your goals and draw contentment into your surroundings.

LOVE & ROMANCE

You can expect great fulfillment as you nurture the emotional qualities of another who appreciate you dearly. This is a time of higher development and great happiness in your life. You may find you have a natural inclination towards the metaphysical and spiritual, as this is a source of sustenance to you. Looking at the broader perspective enables you to put any personal problems into a more comprehensive view, and you gain inner peace and emotional stability. You feel a sense of freedom and liberation, as you are able to enjoy a well-earned break from your everyday routine. All goes brilliantly for you, and you experience the deepening of emotional harmony and well-being in your surroundings. You are an original and visionary individual who draws sublime experiences into your world. You express yourself authentically and genuinely to a significant other who holds considerable meaning for you.

IDEAS & CREATIVITY

Life is likely to get busy, it is time to seize the moment and take advantage of an opportunity which arrives soon. A message or several, are expected to cross your path, and your swift action will help realize the full potential possible. Abundance is ready to blossom in your life. This is a month which sees many pieces of information arrive simultaneously, you find that things flow much faster than the average speed. Good news is likely, and you may even get unexpected offers which heighten your delight. This is a refreshing and rejuvenating time. Expect abundance and variety to give your life a boost. Change is possible, but you will have to think on your feet to quickly evaluate and choose the best direction to suit your needs. Some fantastic news is ready to arrive, and you can enjoy the heightened activity which surrounds you. A busy and hectic environment follows the Full Moon in Libra on the 19th, you swiftly evaluate and manage situations. April is a time which sees you multitasking, going into the various aspects of your life with incredible agility.

There is cleansing which is required, this has you release destructive influences and takes you towards a phase of transformation. Releasing the past guides you towards a new chapter of potential. You are in search of a new adventure, and after several disappointments, new understand arrives which shows you that you are being guided to move in a fresh direction. You possess strengths which are magnetic, capable, and insightful. This helps you deal with hard knocks, and it enhances your ability to expand your horizons as you keep bouncing back, knowing that what didn't work out, wasn't meant to be. You are happiest with a variety of exotic and captivating options, and this has you seek out a path which inspires your imagination. Ultimately you grow and learn, no longer willing to stick to a narrow or precarious track as you can appreciate a broader perspective having gone through past trials

May Horoscope

ASTROLOGICAL THEME & ZODIAC ENERGY

DETERMINED ~ SHREWD~ PROGRESSIVE

WORK & CAREER

This is a month of study, preparation, and planning. Developing your goals involves careful consideration, as significant life changes are available. By going through the process of developing your path carefully, you gain a broad awareness of what you hope to achieve, and the steps necessary to get there. This is a time of taking stock, letting go of projects which haven't reached fruition and preparing for success through methodical and diligent work. As you see your circumstances improving, your wisdom and knowledge enable you to correctly ascertain the correct path forward. You are being guided to develop your skills on all levels, and this acquired knowledge will contribute to you achieving a significant goal later this year. Advancement is possible, and your progress towards *the achievement of goals by surmounting obstacles and resonating personal power.*

LOVE & ROMANCE

You enjoy a heightened sense of harmony, warmth, and abundance. This is a time of positive emotional well-being, and may also reflect the beginning of an exact situation which deepens and becomes more profound. You draw love, compassion, and affection into your world. Your consciousness radiates abundance, and you feel able to trust your inner feelings to guide your path forward with another. Your heart is ruling, and you listen to your intuition which speaks about developing a personal situation in your life. You awaken to the abundance possible and take steps to establish a relationship to a new level of connection. You feel emotional fulfillment, happiness, and warmth. The positive energy created between you and your love leaves you feeling content and joyful. You open your heart up to your partner on a new level and access heightened romantic potential.

IDEAS & CREATIVITY

You gain insight and clarity into a goal you have in mind. This represents the beginning of a journey, and you plan the steps required to put this potential into motion. You feel a sense of raw power as you have made a substantial breakthrough and now can establish a fresh beginning in your life which inspires you. Success is imminent, your mental clarity is providing you with a landscape which is abundant. This is the beginning of a situation which is likely to further your cause, but it is not clear how many hurdles are required to be overcome. This May indicates that great insight and clarity is available to you. Your conscious understanding and mental reasoning are heightened, which makes powerful strategies and plans easier to formulate. This gives you a broader view of what may be possible for you in the future. And after the May 18th Blue Moon in Scorpio, and you feel ready to embrace the potential which seeks to manifest in your life.

ISSUES & HURDLES

You release the hold the past has had on your emotional well-being. You are courageous and determined to succeed. Releasing this pain speaks of advancement in your thinking. You move away from a situation which was limiting your progress. Examining your goals, questioning your path, helps free up options. Releasing the pain puts you on a journey of self-development, and takes you to a new direction. You reveal hidden forces and secrets and are capable of overcoming hurdles as you tap into your inner reservoir of fortitude. You enhance the potential possible by being reflective and understanding the need to release pain and heal. This carries you forward towards an absolute path and has you seeking deeper meaning in your life. Wisdom crystallizes into a plan of action, and you draw raw potential into your surroundings.

June Horoscope

ASTROLOGICAL THEME & ZODIAC ENERGY

INDIVIDUAL ~ PERCEPTIVE ~ WELL-DIRECTED

WORK & CAREER

You have a goal in mind and have to rise up and meet the challenge you face. Using qualities of strength and fortitude you have everything at your disposal which you need to achieve your goals. A test from the universe is asking you to persevere in your quest. There are understanding and guidance available which helps you plot a course of action which will take you to a new chapter in your working life. You may have felt discouraged by a problematic career climate, it is likely you have to dig deep to reach the finish line, but getting it is achievable. If you have run into a detour that has turned into a barrier, take some time to gain insight into how best to overcome that which hold your progress back. Once you understand your situation fully, keep your eyes on the goal, and you'll see it's much closer then you had previously realized.

LOVE & ROMANCE

This is a time of increased harmony and social celebration. You gather with friends and engage in lively and engaging conversations. Your social circle is a warm and abundant, and this brings you a heightened sense of well-being. You enjoy spending time with your friends and can plan towards a specific celebration you have in mind. As you talk about the options available, many ideas and possibilities come to mind. Discussions with others help give you a broader sense of what you hope to achieve, and where your plan is taking you. You draw positive energy into your life, and your emotional well-being is joyful and harmonious. This is a journey which inspires you creatively and provides you with a warm sense of community and connection with others. You are grounded and secure and embrace good times with those you care about. You will likely see improvement in your social life after the Full Moon in Sagittarius on the 17th and enjoy more freedom to socialize and get together with valued friends.

IDEAS & CREATIVITY

This is an inspiring time which utilizes innovative thinking to produce genius results. You don't settle for the traditional approach and embrace your originality with vibrant ideas which you set in motion. You are quick-witted, capable, and daring in achieving your desired results. You feel inspired and exuberant, setting forth with a passion for adventure. You are determined to succeed, and you wear your enthusiasm like a badge of honor. This indicates the initial spark of a new idea which resonates warmly with you is likely. You have the commitment and energy to put your thoughts into action and achieve abundant results. You develop your ideas and visions and make things happen with your can-do attitude. You are self-confident and ready to build your intuition. You can overcome any challenges in your way during this time.

Jupiter at Opposition on June 10th is a time which may heighten your stress levels. This is a journey which makes it difficult to see the finish line. It can bring up painful emotions or take you to dark places, but you dare to face these painful feelings and illuminate that which seeks to be known. You may have subconscious fears which are making you feel insecure, anxiety and doubt may plague your mind on this journey. This is providing insight into your deeper feelings, and as you understand what this energy is trying to teach you, you begin to journey towards higher consciousness. You heighten your perception and become receptive to the secretive power which is making itself known to you. You gain access to your shadow side, and as you become consciously aware of these tendencies towards doubt and insecurity, you are able to release it to the universe and turn it into more positive vibrations, your life picks up a more favorable vibration during and after the June 17th Full Moon in Sagittarius.

July Horoscope

ASTROLOGICAL THEME & ZODIAC ENERGY

CREATIVE ~ ADVENTURESOME ~ GIVING

WORK & CAREER

July is a month which takes you towards significant stability and reward. You have reached a point where you now have the confidence to achieve a high level result in any endeavor you focus your attention towards. You accomplish profound rewards which bring you a sense of satisfaction. There is a sense of peace, harmony, and fulfillment which allows you to feel secure. Your efforts have paid significant reward into your life, and you can enjoy well-deserved success, comfort, and joy. You have the confidence to know that any undertaking you choose to develop will likely succeed, as you have the self-discipline and patience to obtain a successful outcome. You are re-energized, rejuvenated, and enjoy the pleasure which flows into your world. This is a time where you can appreciate abundance, and *create plans for future progress knowing you have what it takes to get there.*

LOVE & ROMANCE

It is time to rejoice and celebrate with friends or family. Your social life is happy and draws a sense of abundance into your world. Relationships are warmhearted, and invitations are highlighted during this month. Spending time with people you value replenishes your energetic system. You are self-assured, confident, and enjoy the psychological balance. You are optimistic, expansive, and thoughtful. You cultivate meaningful relationships and are positively seen by others. This is a valuable time which carefully builds your inner resources and provides you with a happy outlet as you embrace spending time with others and expanding your social circle. You choose your friends with great care, and this enables you to feel in touch with your tribe. Being in alignment with those around you produces energy which is practical and imaginative. Your social situation improves, July highlights are your ability to expand your social circle with new contacts. This occurs after the July 16th Full Moon in Capricorn.

IDEAS & CREATIVITY

This is a month of gaining clarity and insight, it does lead you towards the realization of dreams and aspirations. It is a mystical journey which enchants your soul. You are being guided to gain access to hidden knowledge which will help you develop a broad awareness, this understanding illuminates a compelling solution. You draw abundance into your world, beauty and grace surround you. You can relax and enjoy a deep emotional connection which rejuvenates your energy. This creates the necessary balance in your life, and you draw on these foundations to experience deep fulfillment and happiness. New ideas and projects will be implemented after a time of reflection and introspection. You bring forth ideas which have been brewing inside of you, seeking growth and development. Allowing yourself time to expand this journey heightens the potential available.

ISSUES & HURDLES

You find yourself faced with an obstacle which tests your patience around the time of the July 2nd total Solar Eclipse. You have may some significant issues which have been causing you sleepless nights. You are required to look deep within, search under the layers of emotional stress and anxiety, and tune into what you hope to achieve. You can trust your intuition to guide you but spending time honestly evaluating your situation will give you the unique wisdom required. This heads you toward an awakening of spirit as listening to your heart provides you with fresh information which is innately valuable. If you find yourself struggling at this point in time, understand that this sense of disquiet is required to reveal a new chapter of potential in your life. Help is available from the universe, spending time planning goals will likely show the correct course of action, which will take yo towards fulfillment and happiness.

August Horoscope

ASTROLOGICAL THEME & ZODIAC ENERGY

DETERMINED ~ SUCCESSFUL ~ MAGNETIC

WORK & CAREER

A new beginning beckons, this inspires you to expand your horizons and set off on a fresh adventure. You make strides towards achieving your goals and seek out fresh challenges. Discovering your life's purpose will help you act on your aspirations. A burst of inspiration gives you the confidence required to head in a new direction. An endeavor you are involved with begins to take on a life of its own, you push past fear and embrace uncertainty, knowing it will take you towards uncharted territories. A whole new world of possibilities opens up, and you discover you are able to achieve more by being open to a variety of options. Your thoughts become intentions which quickly manifest into being, providing you with positive outcomes. It may appear to some that you fess effortlessly achieve your goals but plenty of planning and hard work gets you there as well as good luck, you see visible improvement in your working life after the August 15th Full Moon in Aquarius. Choose the opportunity that is in alignment with your vision, as that one is meant for you to develop.

LOVE & ROMANCE

Your cup fills over with the bounty which is contained in the gifts which enter your life. This is a journey of abundance, and you feel well catered for, your emotional needs are met, and you feel blessed by the beauty which enters your life. You see the potential which is available in your world, and you cultivate kindness towards others while keeping in mind the higher goals you hope to achieve. Your imagination is heightened, you display empathy and emotional understanding which positively impacts your circumstances. Pulling all parts of your life together you find your situation is lively and expansive, offering you many opportunities to enjoy and celebrate life. This is a time which symbolizes knowledge, vitality and good fortune and provides you with promises of success and achievement. You glimpse the potential possible as you head towards your goals.

IDEAS & CREATIVITY

Your intuition is guiding you to make some decisive changes in your life. You confront challenges and reinvent your life through the cleansing action of change. You have the necessary patience and understanding to reflect and go within. This enables you to access highly developed sensitivity and empathetic abilities. You gain clarity and a sense of purpose which allows you to move outside of your comfort zone and glimpse the unlimited possibilities which entice you towards change. You attract and draw strong energies into your environment, this provides you with a variety of options. Excitement and adventure swirl around you and this is a result of forces springing up from deep within your nature. You have surmounted hurdles and now know the unique power of your self-worth. You are being guided towards developing your life and obtaining spiritual meaning which helps you evolve to a fresh chapter of potential.

Significant change is indicated, tearing down old layers which no longer serve your purpose, enables you to form a new foundation. Things may have felt uncertain recently, you have gone through a trial which has affected your heart. Cutting swiftly through the issues which have clung to your spirit recently will allow you to reach a new area to develop. You are on the verge of making necessary changes in your life, and this does involve leaving something behind. There may be dreams you have built which are no longer capable of being developed. This is a time of transition and change, as you are required to release the past and move forward in a new area. You are moving towards a new world, and while it is essential to process the emotions this transition bring up, you can have a faith you are being drawn to a better situation.

September Horoscope

CURIOUS ~ DEDICATED ~ UNIQUE

WORK & CAREER

You are headed towards a fresh beginning, and this has the potential to completely rejuvenate your life. A sense of adventure and excitement emerges as you embark on this innovative journey. The winds of change seek to enter your realm. There may be something that you want to change your life, and the opportunity is now approaching to take tangible steps which will see you embark on a new chapter of development. Adjustments may be needed along the way, so maintaining a flexible outlook will help facilitate long-term growth. To step forward towards this dream, you may have to leave something behind. Travel is indicated, there is a sense that you are about to embark on a significant journey which develops your life on multiple levels. Keep your goals in mind, one step at a time leads to a *bigger and brighter future, opportunities are likely to arrive which help keep you motivated along the way. You have what it takes to access an unlimited bounty. Stay balanced, be confident, and continue to head towards the realization of your dreams.*

LOVE & ROMANCE

You are logical and decisive, able to spot the opportunity which arrives on your doorstep and begin to be developed. You are quick thinking, quick acting, and ready to lead forth on a journey of discovery. You seek stimulating conversations and a social life which engages your senses and captivates your attention. You have an independent spirit and enjoy your own freedom, you feel tempted to expand your horizons and embrace change in your life. This is an excellent time to ask yourself, what do I need progress with, what do I hope to transform in my life. Your intuition is likely to guide you to the right area to develop. You are being tempted to get out of your comfort zone and meet new characters who inspire you. You combine strategy with emotional awareness and dare to make substantial changes. When you head in a direction which calls to your passion, you find the momentum of inspiration arrives to allow you to commit to a course of action.

IDEAS & CREATIVITY

A specific approach is necessary, and being firm and logical enables you to assert your power and overcome any hurdles which interfere with your progress. You are being led to a better situation, and understanding what to do next will be pivotal correctly making the best decision for your job. It is essential to utilize a mental strategy to understand your goals and form a plan to get there. This enables you to harness your personal magic, and develop your goals efficiently. You are on the right path, just focus on the steps, take the time necessary to think about where you are headed from here. The universe is forcing you to be creative in finding a workable solution. A revelation is likely, but a pause for contemplation is required to uncover fresh information which will assist you in developing your goals.

This thing may have been unsettling or uncertain recently. There may have been confusion in your life which left you wondering where you stand in regards to another person or situation. Utilizing your insight, you can now cut swiftly through the ambiguity and reach the heart of the matter. Things may suddenly crystallize and appear clear as you gain access to hidden knowledge. On a broader level this month links you to feelings of déjà vu, strange coincidences and feelings of synchronicity are likely. You may even have a sense that destiny has brought you to this point in your journey, and now a decision is required to efficiently develop the correct path. A swift approach is needed, cutting away from the past reveals a fresh layer of potential. As you admit the truth, you understand exactly what you need in your life to succeed on this September.

October Horoscope

ASTROLOGICAL THEME & ZODIAC ENERGY

TALENTED ~ OBSERVANT ~ INSPIRATIONAL

WORK & CAREER

You find a conversation with a supportive person in your life helps you obtain knowledge and perception which allows you to recognize the potential which flows into this situation. This person is someone who symbolizes intellect, communication, information, and personal magic. You feel empowered by the sense of understanding which engaging with this shrewd character brings to your life. You are inventive, adaptable, and problem-solving and this helps you use your wits to overcome tactical issues. There is an opportunity to act just at the right moment to develop this venture. You are daring, capable, and expensive. You recognize limitations and overcome them with ingenious solutions. This takes you on an imaginative and adventurous journey and results in living your dreams and enjoying all that life has to offer.

Love & Romance

You are curious, and dedicate yourself to the process of understanding your needs. You display energy which is wise, your spirit is taking you towards further self-development. You may feel triggered by intense emotions such as anxiety, and doubt, but when you dig a little deeper, you understand you are being guided to focus on developing a fresh vision. This is a challenging path, and you may be faced with having to overcome hurdles and remove limitations. Sticking to your goals and maintaining a flexible outlook, allows you to adjust course as necessary. You express perceptive and insightful energy, you follow your instincts freely, evolve your dreams, and are in tune with your inner needs. Your sensitivity and compassion make you someone others are drawn to. Your ability to tap into the heart of the matter, allows you to understand the inner workings of situations around you.

IDEAS & CREATIVITY

This is a time of stability and growth in your life. You complete goals, achieve success, and are able to appreciate the abundance which results from the hard work you have put in. You are able to recognize the bigger picture and focus on building foundations which provides you with increased security. You work patiently and diligently, not finding the process of creating your dream tedious or boring. You value set goals and know you have what it takes to last the distance with any idea you set your mind to. There are exciting kinds of opportunities set to appear in your world, which give you the chance to improve your surroundings. You may even find you have a lucky break in romance, and you embrace the idea of sharing your abundance with another. Your heart is open, and this is allowing the heightened potential to emerge in your life. There are some exciting changes ahead, and you will see how capable you are, and how many talents you have to offer.

You find you have the strength to power through to a new chapter of potential in your world. It does test your fortitude, it brings up uncomfortable emotions which require you to process and deal with as these feelings as they risk destabilizing your progress if left to fester. It is not an easy time, personal growth and achievement are achieved through a process of transformation. This sees you harness your emotional strength to continue to work towards the realization of your goals. Significant change is indicated, and you have the self-discipline, patience, courage, and compassion to deal with any hurdles or issues which cross your path. Your will represents your inner strength and gives you the power to overcome problems. You know you can endure life's obstacles by drawing on your inner strength with confidence and persistence.

November Horoscope

ASTROLOGICAL THEME & ZODIAC ENERGY

SELECTIVE ~ INSIGHTFUL ~ PRECISE

WORK & CAREER

You gather assistance from a valuable source. Someone you hold in high regard is able to give you advice and help you develop your career goals. Significant change is achieved through the acquisition of wisdom. This authority figure provides you with a solid foundation to allow you to continue to work towards your goals. This person is someone who represents power and authority, they represent structure and stability. Going to this person for guidance allows you to create order out of chaos by carefully building a structure to your ideas. This person is a strategic thinker who is highly organized and coordinated, they are able to help you achieve your goals in the physical realm. You establish order in your world by paying attention to specific guidelines and rules. You may find your

*creativity is restricted but only while you are
working towards the gaining of wisdom.*

LOVE & ROMANCE ND

*A time of emotional harmony and abundance is
approaching. Someone in your life brings you great
joy, this person truly understands who you are as an
individual and respects and admires your talents.
They believe in you and see you as someone who is
special and unique. This is a time which enables you
to take the time to get to know this person accurately
and you find that they also have some extraordinary
qualities which captivate your imagination. This is a
journey into the realm of emotions, and you see there
is definite potential to turn this fantastic partnership
into a significant situation. You may discover that it
requires a lot more commitment then initially
appears on the surface. It is time to take a risk and
begin the steps which will build stable foundations
for future progress. You recognize this situation as
blessing and treat it with gratitude and an open
heart. This is a time of personal development which
brings you great happiness. Blocked energy is
removed during the Leonids Meteor Shower on*

November 17th and 18th, this sees an improvement in your own life occur shortly afterward.

IDEAS & CREATIVITY

Fortune is shining down brightly on you at this time. You enter a very auspicious time for building new foundations, this is leading you toward a fresh start on a new chapter of potential. This is a fabulous time, and an opportunity arrives in the second half of the month which begins a new phase of your life. The kind of opportunity which is available to you includes the chance to improve your financial picture, and may even be the lucky break you have been searching for. Keep expanding your horizons so you may make the discovery that is seeking to enter your life. This is likely to be something you have waited for, and you will view it as essential and understand the implications involved. You are clear in your intentions, and this provides you with the ability to make the most of the incredible flow of potential which is set to sweep into your life.

Duties, responsibilities, and additional tasks arrive which demand your attention. You shouldn't have to shoulder the extra workload, so look for ways to delegate jobs which would allow you to take a breather. It's also important to pace yourself this month, as finding your rhythm will let you keep moving forward without risking burnout. The good news is once the additional tasks are dealt with, life will return to normal, and there will even be opportunities to unwind and relax with friends. This allows you to re-balance your energy after a hectic time which has been demanding. You have what it takes to have a productive time, and the extra work may even lead to a surprising opportunity which arrives to spark your interest. It's time to focus on the tasks at hand and carry on until the work is done.

December Horoscope

ASTROLOGICAL THEME & ZODIAC ENERGY

CHARMING ~ ACCEPTING ~ SECURE

WORK & CAREER

You soon find you are at the top of your game and this helps you conjure up a fantastic opportunity to express your talents in. You shine in your social circle and can get ready for a hectic time ahead. There is much to accomplish, and it is an auspicious time to put plans into place for future progress. As you start thinking about your hopes and dreams, you draw blessings from the universe which help you to solve issues and get working towards goals. You plant the seeds for future progress and begin to make plans for the next phase of life. While there may be some confusion at this time, you are being guided to sweep away old concepts and develop your world in progressive ways. Your inquisitiveness and curiosity have you go through remarkable changes and developments. Great adventures are ready for you to embark on. A welcome surprise arrives to guide this process.

LOVE & ROMANCE

You may be feeling unusually reflective and nostalgic soon. Old feelings you haven't fully processed may emerge, especially ones relating to change and letting go. There is positive energy seeking to make itself known to you which will help you heal. This emboldens you to make a transition into a new area of life. This could lead to a breakthrough which sees you prioritize self-care. A welcome opportunity is also set to arrive soon. Your personal magic helps create energy which sees you take a plunge towards a fresh area to develop. There may be some significant soul-searching involved, you can remove blocks and doubt and expand your horizons. This new direction consists of meeting kindred spirits which reminds you how much you value social connection. You channel your creative energy into an area which makes you happy and stirs your passion for life.

IDEAS & CREATIVITY

There is an undercurrent of exciting growth which surrounds your potential. You may feel an irresistible call towards self-expression, this sees you preparing for an awakening, allow space to process any heavy emotions which emerge and arrange for increased momentum towards a new area which inspires you greatly. Stimulating ideas provide you with the stimulus to transform your world. This sees you get involved in a new venture to develop. Incredible changes are noted for you, you'll get much accomplished if you attend to unfinished projects first before embarking on a new venture which arrives to inspire you soon. An opportunity next month gives you a fantastic chance to reinvent yourself, which could send you in an entirely new direction. Invites arrive out of the blue for dynamic and spontaneous adventures out with friends. Creativity is heightened which activates innovative thinking.

This is a journey which involves some anxiety making itself known to your consciousness. You may be building up your courage and confidence to expand your horizons into an area which is outside of your comfort zone. This can bring some tension and drama into your life, and you may fear that you will end up going straight back to the beginning without having achieved your goals. Even if you aren't feeling as hopeful as you had been in the past, you can continue, utilizing your mental clarity to understand that fear and doubt only seek to hold you back. If you believe that powerful forces are on your side, things will surely work out for you.

Maintaining an optimistic attitude will allow you to release the troublesome vibrations which arise as you embark on a new area in your life. It's natural that there may be some unresolved feelings from the past that need to be dealt with, introspection will provide you with the clarity needed to move forward. The December 22nd Solstice sees a blocked situation in your life is drawing to a close. The removal of old energy will create a position that allows new opportunities to enter into your life.

54

ASTROLOGICAL

EVENTS

2019

Astrological Events
2019

Astrological Events
2019

All time is set in Coordinated Universal Time Zone (UT±0)

January Astrology

January 3, 4 - Quadrantids Meteor Shower.

The Quadrantids meteor shower run yearly from January 1-5. The Quadrantids meteor shower peaks this year on the night of the 3rd and morning of the 4th.

This meteor shower enables you to remove old energy from around your creative processes. This is an excellent time to cleanse yourself from blocked energy, realign your chakras, and open yourself up to fresh ideas and innovative solutions. Set an intention to let go of that which has been holding your progress back and keeping your energy stuck. By consciously admitting that you need to refine your goals, dreams, and desires, you allow your creative energy to focus on areas that bring you the highest reward, while simultaneously letting go of the ideas which have failed to reach fruition in your life. The universe loves an abyss, and this process of letting go, and burning away outworn ideas, is fundamentally important in manifesting new opportunities into your life.

January 6 - New Moon in Capricorn.

The Moon is on the same side of the Earth as the Sun and won't be seen in the night sky. This moon phase occurs at 01:28 UTC. This is an excellent time to observe galaxies and star clusters as there is no moonlight.

This is a time of transformation and change as creative insight opens during this New Moon, and you become more aware how to expand opportunities into your life. This relates to developing your skills to a higher level to open up exciting opportunities for growth. There is excellent potential present reaching you during this time and you are guided along the way by supportive energy

January 6 - Venus with Greatest Western Elongation.

The planet Venus reaches it's highest eastern elongation of 47 degrees from the Sun.

January 6 - Partial Solar Eclipse.

A partial solar eclipse occurs as the Moon hides part of the Sun. This partial solar eclipse occurs in parts of eastern Asia and the northern Pacific Ocean.

This Astrological event is deeply interwoven with the concept of darkness and reawakening. The energy presented represents you being in a state of hibernation, and deep within you, creativity stirs. Your spirit is going through a process of metamorphosis, so you are transforming. Old energy is removed during the eclipse, and this sees you reborn through the shedding of old skins. You are ready for new growth in your life, embrace a new beginning.

January 14 – First Quarter Moon in Aries.

This Moon phase occurs at 06.45 UTC.

January 21 - Full Moon in Leo, Supermoon.

This full moon phase occurs at 05:16 UTC. This full moon is called the Full Wolf Moon because this was the time of year when hungry wolf packs howled outside camps. This full moon has also been known as the Old Moon and the Moon After Yule. This is the first of three super-moons for 2019.

January 21 - Total Lunar Eclipse.

This total lunar eclipse occurs in the majority of North America, South America, eastern Pacific Ocean, as well as the western Atlantic Ocean, extreme western Europe, and West Africa.

The total Lunar Eclipse guides you to a place of stillness where you can see things more clearly and obtain inner harmony and increased happiness. This process takes you on a mysterious journey towards enlightenment and allows you to develop a deeper connection with the divine light that is your source. This draws feelings of joy, belonging, and emotional well-being into your life.

January 22 - Conjunction of Venus and Jupiter.

A conjunction of Venus and Jupiter takes place on January 22. The two bright planets will be within 2.4 degrees of each other in the pre-dawn sky.

January 27 – Last Quarter Moon in Scorpio.

This Moon phase occurs at 21.10 UTC.

February Astrology

February 4 - New Moon in Aquarius.

The Moon is on the same side of the Earth as the Sun and will not be visible in the night sky. This phase occurs at 21:03 UTC. This is an excellent time to view galaxies and stars as there is no moonlight to obscure your view of the universe.

Heightened insight, perception is available during this New Moon. This illuminates your energy with radiant potential. You are transforming your horizons in a direction that is in alignment with your core values. This is likely to soon lead to an inspiring, creative, and enriching time for you with exciting surprises in store

February 12 – First Quarter Moon in Taurus.
This Moon phase occurs at 22.26 UTC.

February 19 - Full Moon in Leo, Supermoon.

The Moon is on the opposite side of the Earth as the Sun and will be fully illuminated. This phase occurs at 15:53 UTC. This full moon is known as the Full Snow Moon because the heaviest snows usually fall during this month. Since hunting is difficult, this full moon has also been recognized as the Full Hunger Moon, since the harsh weather made fishing difficult. This is also the second of three super-moons for 2019. The Moon will be at its nearest approach to the Earth and will look slightly larger and brighter than usual.

February 26 – Last Quarter Moon in Sagittarius.

This Moon phase occurs at 11.28 UTC.

February 27 - Mercury at largest Eastern Elongation.

The planet Mercury reaches an eastern elongation of 18.1 degrees from the Sun.

March Astrology

March 5 – Mercury Retrograde begins in Pisces.

During a retrograde period, it isn't the right time to move forward in any practical venture. Be prepared for misunderstandings and miscommunications to be prevalent.

You may be feeling isolated and restricted during the retrograde, but this is an excellent time to listen to your inner voice, as you will receive empowering energy which will help inspire you creatively and allow you to push through barriers to achieve abundance in your personal world. This will direct you to complete fulfillment and wholeness in your life. Make plans during this time but put them into action after the retrograde ends.

March 6 - New Moon in Pisces.

The Moon is on the same side of the Earth as the Sun and will not be visible in the night sky. This phase occurs at 16:04 UTC. This is an excellent time to observe galaxies and stars because there is no moonlight to interfere.

During this New Moon phase, you benefit from enhanced fortuitous energy, which is perfect for embracing family connections and feeling blessed by the gifts in your life. This New Moon allows you to clear negativity, and feel a sense of complete happiness.

March 14 – First Quarter Moon in Gemini.

This Moon phase occurs at 10.27 UTC.

March 20 - March Equinox.

The March equinox takes place at 21:58 UTC. The Sun be shining on the equator, and there will be equal amounts of day and night throughout the world. This is the first day of spring (vernal equinox) in the Northern Hemisphere.

March 21 - Full Moon in Libra, Supermoon.

This full Moon is on the opposite side of the Earth as the Sun and shall be fully illuminated. This phase occurs at 01:43 UTC. This full moon is known as the Full Worm Moon because this was the time of year when the ground would soften, and earthworms would reappear. This full moon is also known as the Full Crow Moon, the Full Crust Moon, the Full Sap Moon, and the Lenten Moon. This is also the last of three super-moons for 2019. The Moon will be close to the Earth and will look slightly larger and brighter than usual.

March 28 – Last Quarter Moon in Capricorn.

This Moon phase occurs at 22.26 UTC. April 15 –

March 28 - Mercury Retrograde ends in Pisces.

You can now move forward with any delayed plans that you have been putting off due to the Mercury Retrograde phase. Relationships should soon improve as tensions ease.

You are about to enter an exciting new phase of inner awakening. This is the perfect time to start fresh in new endeavors and activities and to take the next step in your personal development. Relationships are unfolding and crystallizing into more profound vitality. You are urged to seek a new adventure, and begin journeying towards greater prosperity and happiness. Feel an overwhelming sense of wonder as you visualize your desires becoming a reality.

April Astrology

April 5 - New Moon in Aries.

The New Moon is on the same side of the Earth as the Sun and will not be visible in the night sky. This moon phase occurs at 08:51 UTC. This is an excellent time to observe galaxies and stars because there is no moonlight visible.

A broad river of healing energy flows toward you during this New Moon. This powerful emotional flow of sentiment is directed at you to allow you to heal the past. It brings you in touch with deep reservoirs of sentimentality, allowing wholeness and harmony to pervade in your life. You resonate the energy reaching you, and this will enable you to radiate grace and emotional wholeness to those around you.

April 11 - Mercury at most substantial Western Elongation.

The planet Mercury reaches its most substantial western elongation of 27.7 degrees from the Sun.

April 12 – First Quarter Moon in Cancer.

This Moon phase occurs at 19.06 UTC.

April 19 - **Full Moon in Libra.**

The Moon is on the opposite side of the Earth as the Sun and will be completely illuminated. This moon phase occurs at 11:12 UTC. This full moon is known as Full Pink Moon because it marked an appearance of the first spring flowers. This full moon has also been known as the Sprouting Grass Moon, the Growing Moon, and the Egg Moon. Many coastal areas call it Full Fish Moon because this was the time the fish swam upriver to breed.

April 22, 23 - **Lyrids Meteor Shower.**

The Lyrids meteor shower runs each year from April 16-25. This meteor shower peaks on the night of the 22nd and the morning of the 23rd. These meteors sometimes produce bright dust trails that last for several seconds.

There is incredible energy coming to you from the Universe. These vibrations are the powers that shape matter, as they resonate the element of fire that has been stabilized into clarity. This relates to improved insight, ideas, and creativity. You can tap into this kind of energy to give form to your creative goals as it does allow you a heightened ability to manifest your desires in the physical realm.

April 26 – Last Quarter Moon in Aquarius.

This Moon phase occurs at 22.18 UTC.

May Astrology

May 4 - New Moon in Taurus.

The Moon will be located on the same side of the Earth as the Sun and won't be seen in the night sky. This phase occurs at 22:46 UTC. The new moon phase is a brilliant time to observe galaxies and stars because there is no moonlight visible.

This New Moon signifies fresh hope, abundance, and inspiration. It connects you with knowing your place in the world and feeling a strong bond with others. This safety net is reassuring and enables you to develop your life knowing that you are supported and valued.

May 6, 7 - Eta Aquarids Meteor Shower.

The Eta Aquarids meteor shower runs annually from April 19 to May 28. It peaks this year on the night of May 6 and the morning of the May 7.

This Meteor shower signals that a reawakening or change of direction will soon take place which leads you towards a new venture. You are being guided to keep your faith active and trust in your natural instincts, knowing that you will be guided towards a place of opportunity and personal growth. Follow your heart, and realize that by engaging in mindfulness, you resonate positive attributes, and radiate boundless and vibrant joy.

May 12 – First Quarter Moon in Leo.

This Moon phase occurs at 01.12 UTC.

May 18 - Full Moon in Scorpio, Blue Moon.

The Moon is on the opposite side of the Earth as the Sun, and its face will be fully illuminated. This phase occurs at 21:11 UTC. The May full moon is known as the Full Flower Moon because this was the time of year when spring flowers are in abundance. This full moon is also known as the Full Corn Planting Moon and the Milk Moon. This year there is also a blue moon. This unusual calendar event only happens once every few years, giving rise to the term, "once in a blue moon." There are usually three full moons in each season. A fourth full moon is called a Blue moon and occurs on average once every 2.7 years.

This Blue Moon reflects your journey towards obtaining profound insights. This symbolizes your personal quest towards enlightenment. As you isolate yourself from the preoccupations of the masses, you create a sense of entering the wilderness to learn more about your highest self. This brings you a sense of oneness with the immeasurable and infinite that is your source and has the fantastic ability to re-balance and ground your energy.

May 26 – Last Quarter Moon in Aquarius.

This Moon phase occurs at 16.33 UTC.

June Astrology

June 3 - New Moon in Gemini.

The Moon is on the same side of the Earth as the Sun and will not be visible in the night sky. This moon phase occurs at 10:02 UTC. This is an excellent time to observe galaxies and stars because there is no moonlight to interfere.

This New Moon sees you transforming your horizons as you feed and nourish that which brings you joy, yo help to manifest a life that is lived more thoroughly and is in alignment with your core values. You are healing on all levels, and this nourishes hidden parts of your soul.

June 10 – First Quarter Moon in Virgo.

This Moon phase occurs at 05.59 UTC.

June 10 - Jupiter at Opposition.

The planet Jupiter will be at its nearest approach to Earth, and its planet face will be illuminated entirely by the Sun.

June 17 - Full Moon in Sagittarius.

The Full Moon is on the opposite side of the Earth a the Sun, and its face will be completely illuminated. This moon phase occurs at 08:31 UTC. This full mo is known as Full Strawberry Moon because it is the peak of strawberry harvesting season. The June Full Moon has also been known as the Full Rose Moon and the Full Honey Moon.

June 21 - June Solstice.

The June solstice occurs at 15:54 UTC. The North Pole will be tilted toward the Sun, which, having reached its northernmost position in the sky will be over the Tropic of Cancer at 23.44 degrees north latitude. This heralds the first day of summer (summer solstice) in the Northern Hemisphere, and is considered one of the most influential times of the year for many traditional cultures.

This Solstice sees some incredible energy entering your life. It has the essence of radiance and will fill your life with brilliance and regeneration. Your passion is likely to be ignited by a new project, and as this endeavor expands into realization, energizing creativity brings with it an overwhelming sense of vibrancy and clarity that burns away any fear or doubts you may have about moving forward.

June 23 - Mercury at largest Eastern Elongation.

The planet Mercury reaches most substantial eastern elongation of 25.2 degrees from the Sun.

June 25 – Last Quarter Moon in Aries.

This Moon phase occurs at 09.46 UTC.

July Astrology

July 2 - New Moon in Cancer.

The July New Moon is located on the same side of the Earth as the Sun and won't be visible in the night sky. This moon phase occurs at 19:16 UTC. This is an excellent time to observe galaxies and stars because there is no moonlight visible.

You may find yourself feeling restless as you question your place in the world. As you see the sliver of light in the New Moon, you feel a sense of positive feedback from the universe, that you are on the right path to achieving your goals. Your dreams often appear tantalizingly just out of reach, making you question if you are headed in the right direction. You have asked the divine for guidance and signs of communication, and the mysterious lunar energy materializes to provide clarity.

July 2 - Total Solar Eclipse.

The total solar eclipse occurs in parts of the southern Pacific Ocean, central Chile, and central Argentina. A partial eclipse is visible in the Pacific Ocean and western South America.

July 7 – Mercury Retrograde begins in Leo.

During a retrograde period, it isn't the right time to move forward in any practical venture. Be prepared for misunderstandings and miscommunications to be prevalent.

You may be feeling isolated and restricted during the retrograde, but this is an excellent time to go within, as you will receive empowering energy which will help inspire you creatively and allow you to push through barriers to achieve abundance in your world. This will direct you to complete fulfillment and wholeness in your life. Make plans during this time but put them into action after the retrograde ends.

July 9 – First Quarter Moon in Libra.

This Moon phase occurs at 10.55 UTC.

July 9 - Saturn at Opposition.

The beautiful ringed planet Saturn will be at its nearest approach to Earth, and it will be illuminated by the Sun.

The planet Saturn's incredible rings illuminate that you are undergoing a time of transformation, where one cycle ends, and you begin to transition into the next phase of your life. You will soon start to see some changes occurring around you that suggest to you the correct path. There is a magical element to this fortuitous energy, which enables opportunities to manifest around you, guiding you towards good fortune. You are destined to develop emotionally and spiritually during this time.

July 16 - Full Moon in Capricorn.

The July Full Moon is located on the opposite side of the Earth as the Sun and will be fully illuminated. This phase occurs at 21:38 UTC. This full moon is known as Full Buck Moon because the male buck deer start to grow new antlers. This full moon is also known as the Full Thunder Moon and the Full Hay Moon.

July 16 - Partial Lunar Eclipse.

The partial lunar eclipse will be visible throughout most of Europe, Africa, central Asia, and the Indian Ocean.

July 25 – Last Quarter Moon in Taurus.

This Moon phase occurs at 01.18 UTC.

July 28, 29 - Delta Aquarids Meteor Shower.

The Delta Aquarids meteor shower peaks on the night of July 28 and morning of July 29.

This meteor shower enables you to remove old energy from around your creative processes. This is an excellent time to cleanse yourself from blocked energy, realign your chakras, and open yourself up to fresh ideas and innovative solutions. Set an intention to let go of that which has been holding your progress back and keeping your energy stuck. By consciously admitting that you need to refine your goals, dreams, and desires, you allow your creative energy to realign towards areas that bring you joy. Burn away outworn or outdated ideas from your consciousness, as this is fundamentally important in manifesting new opportunities into your life.

July 31 - Mercury Retrograde ends in Cancer.

You can now move forward with any delayed plans that you have been putting off due to the Mercury Retrograde phase. Relationships should soon improve as tensions ease.

This is the perfect time to start fresh in new endeavor and activities and to take the next step in your personal development. It is time to transform and grow in your path and appreciate the good things tha you have in your life. The ending of Mercury Retrograde epitomizes emotional evolution, spiritual growth, and heightened emotional perception. Relationships unfold and crystallize into more profound vitality.

August Astrology

August 1 - New Moon in Leo.

The Moon will be on the same side of the Earth as the Sun and will not be visible in the night sky. This moon phase occurs at 03:12 UTC. This is an excellent time to observe galaxies and stars because there is no moonlight to interfere.

The energy you receive from this Full Moon is versatile, adaptive, and graceful. You embrace challenges with the flexibility that few can equal, allowing the rhythm and flow of your life to direct you and bring you more stability. This is a time which symbolizes luck and expansion for you. This generally indicates that harmonious change will soon bring good fortune and enrichment into your life.

August 7 – First Quarter Moon in Scorpio.

This Moon phase occurs at 17.31 UTC.

August 9 - Mercury at most substantial Western Elongation.

The planet Mercury reaches greatest western elongation of 19.0 degrees from the Sun.

August 12, 13 - Perseids Meteor Shower.

The Perseids meteor shower runs each year from July 17 to August 24. It peaks this year on the night of August 12 and the morning of August 13.

A meteor shower enables you to remove old energy from around your creative processes. This is a time where you need to ground and center yourself to find a place of calmness. Only then will you be able to be still in the eye of the storm. This helps you obtain perception and insight into any issues that crop up. There is lots of activity that is hectic around you, and you may feel events are catapulting out of control, as things move quickly forward. You may feel dizzy by some of this sudden movement, and you should prepare by centering yourself and staying grounded during the meteor shower.

August 15 - Full Moon in Aquarius.

The August Full Moon is located on the opposite side of the Earth as the Sun and will be fully illuminated. This phase occurs at 12:30 UTC. The August full moon is known as the Full Sturgeon Moon because sturgeon fish of the Great Lakes and other major lake were quickly caught during this time. This full moon has also been known as the Green Corn Moon and the Grain Moon.

August 23 – Last Quarter Moon in Taurus.

This Moon phase occurs at 14.56 UTC.

August 30 - New Moon in Virgo.

The Moon is on the same side of the Earth as the Sun and will not be visible in the night sky. This moon phase occurs at 10:37 UTC. This is an excellent time to view galaxies and stars because there is no moonlight to interfere.

This New Moon taps into your search for happiness and shows you what can be achieved by nourishing your inner garden. Your inspiration, insight, and creativity come from a sensitive, intuitive place. You are susceptible to the slightest whisper of intuitive feelings, and this makes your creative energy mysterious, hypnotic, dreamlike, and introspective. Your open and reflective, emotional outlook make you a channel for dreams, imagination, and inspiration. Become a hollow chamber that is the conduct of inspired creative energy, as your instinctive sensitivity and inner perception receive power from the subtle essence of the New Moon. This allows you to sense the reality below the surface, and it helps guide you toward knowing which way to channel your creative expression.

September Astrology

September 9 - Neptune at Opposition.

The giant blue planet will be at its closest approach to Earth, and its face will be illuminated by the Sun.

September 6 – First Quarter Moon in Sagittarius.

This Moon phase occurs at 03.10 UTC.

September 14 - Full Moon in Pisces.

The September full Moon is on the opposite side of the Earth as the Sun, and its face will be fully illuminated. This phase occurs at 04:34 UTC. This full moon is known as the Full Corn Moon because the corn is harvested around this time. This full moon is also called the Harvest Moon which is the full moon that occurs nearest to the September equinox each year.

September 22 – Last Quarter Moon in Gemini

This Moon phase occurs at 02.41 UTC.

September 23 - September Equinox.

The 2019 September equinox occurs at 07:50 UTC. The Sun shines directly on the equator, creating equ amounts of day and night throughout the world. This is also the first day of fall (autumnal equinox) in the northern hemisphere and is considered a significant zodiac event for many traditional cultures.

September 28 - New Moon in Virgo.

The Moon is on the same side of the Earth as the Sun and will not be visible in the night sky. This phase occurs at 18:26 UTC. This is an excellent time to observe galaxies and stars because there is no moonlight visible.

October Astrology

October 8 - Draconids Meteor Shower.

The Draconids meteor shower runs annually from October 6-10 and peaks this year on the night of the 8th.

You radiate spectacular creative energy during this meteor shower, which results in dazzling inspiration, ideas, and artistic brilliance. This ignites a passion that surprises you and propels you towards goals with accuracy and confidence. You can set plans in place with confidence, and allow yourself to express intensely creative ideas. Harnessing talents of innovation enable you to capture the energy of manifestation. You radiate the positive power of fire combining vitality with determination. Goals and aspirations set in motion this meteor shower are like to blossom successfully, and soon become ready for further development

October 5 – First Quarter Moon in Capricorn

This Moon phase occurs at 16.47 UTC.

October 13 - Full Moon in Aries.

The October full Moon is on the opposite side of the Earth as the Sun, and its face will be fully illuminate This phase occurs at 21:09 UTC. This full moon is known as the Hunters Moon because at this time of year the leaves are falling, and the game is ready. This full moon is also known as the Travel Moon and the Blood Moon.

October 20 - Mercury at Greatest Eastern Elongation.

The planet Mercury reaches greatest eastern elongation of 24.6 degrees from the Sun.

October 21 – Last Quarter Moon in Cancer.

This Moon phase occurs at 12.39 UTC.

October 21, 22 - Orionids Meteor Shower.

The Orionids meteor shower runs yearly from October 2 to November 7. Orionids meteor shower peaks this year on the night of October 21 and the morning of October 22.

This meteor shower invigorates you with inspired thinking and increased self-confidence. Feelings of brilliance, power, and higher consciousness help guide your path. Insight combines with innovative thinking to help you harness the power of creative ideas. As you give form to your visualizations, you combine fire energy with grounded earthiness. This represents heaven and earth coming together as a source of cosmic energy contained within you

October 27 - Uranus at Opposition.

The planet Uranus will be at its nearest approach to Earth, and its face will be illuminated by the Sun.

October 28 - New Moon in Scorpio.

The Moon will be on the same side of the Earth as the Sun and will not be seen in the night sky. This moon phase occurs at 03:39 UTC. This is an excellent time of the month to view galaxies and stars because there is no moonlight visible.

October 31 – Mercury Retrograde begins in Scorpio.

During a retrograde period, it isn't the right time to move forward in any practical venture. Be prepared for misunderstandings and miscommunications to b prevalent.

Worry and anxiety can be problematic for you this Mercury Retrograde. You may feel as though things are in limbo. It is essential to understand that mercury retrograde can create shadows in your confidence. You are encouraged to release this anxiety, and maintain equilibrium during this time, focusing on self-care. A luxury spa treatment or meditation can do wonders for your spirit.

November Astrology

November 4 – First Quarter Moon in Aquarius.

This Moon phase occurs at 10.23 UTC.

November 5, 6 - Taurids Meteor Shower.

The Taurids meteor shower runs yearly from September 7 to December 10. It peaks this year on the night of November 5.

Burn baby burn! A meteor shower enables you to remove old energy from your life. Banish fear, doubt, and trepidation. This is an excellent time to release blocked energy, and realign your vision to the direction you seek to head towards. It is an excellent time for making plans that you put into place after the mercury retrograde ends.

November 11 - Rare Transit of the planet Mercury Across the Sun.

The planet Mercury moves directly between the Earth and the Sun. This is a rare event that occurs only once every few years. The next transit of Mercury does not take place until 2039.

November 12 - Full Moon in Taurus.

The November full Moon is on the opposite side of the Earth as the Sun, and its face will be fully illuminated. This phase occurs at 13:36 UTC. This full moon is known as Full Beaver Moon as this was the time of year to set beaver traps before the swamps and rivers froze. It is also known as the Frosty Moon and the Hunter's Moon.

November 17, 18 - Leonids Meteor Shower.

The Leonids meteor shower runs yearly from November 6-30. The Leonids meteor shower peaks this year on the night of the 17th and morning of the 18th.

November 19 – Last Quarter Moon in Leo.

This Moon phase occurs at 21.11 UTC.

November 20 - Mercury Retrograde ends in Scorpio.

You can now move forward with any delayed plans that you have been putting off due to the Mercury Retrograde phase. Relationships should soon improve as tensions ease.

You are about to enter an exciting new phase of inner awakening. This is the perfect time to start fresh in new endeavors and activities and to take the next step in your personal development. Relationships are unfolding and crystallizing into more profound vitality. You are urged to seek a new adventure, and begin journeying towards greater prosperity and happiness. Feel an overwhelming sense of wonder as you visualize your desires becoming a reality.

November 24 - Conjunction of Venus and Jupiter.

A conjunction of Venus and Jupiter is visible on November 24. The two planets are within 1.4 degrees of each other in the night sky.

November 26 - New Moon in Scorpio.

The Moon is on the same side of the Earth as the Sun and will not be visible in the night sky. This phase occurs at 15:06 UTC. This is an excellent time to view galaxies and star clusters because there is no moonlight visible.

November 28 - Mercury at Greatest Western Elongation.

The planet Mercury obtains western peak elongation of 20.1 degrees from the Sun.

December Astrology

December 4 – First Quarter Moon in Pisces.

This Moon phase occurs at 06.58 UTC.

December 12 - Full Moon in Gemini.

The Moon is on the opposite side of the Earth as the Sun, and its face will be fully illuminated. This moon phase occurs at 05:14 UTC. This full moon is known as the Full Cold Moon because this is the time of year when the cold winters air arrives and nights become long and dark. This full moon is known as the Long Nights Moon and the Moon Before Yule.

December 13, 14 - Geminids Meteor Shower.

The Geminids meteor shower runs each year from December 7-17. The Geminids meteor showers peak this year on the night of the 13th and morning of the 14th.

This meteor shower urges you to harness its power t burn away old energy and rethink long-held beliefs, allowing you to regain a new perspective. Focus you energy towards optimism, vitality, and personal development. This helps harness the law of attraction, and it paves your way towards a creative and fulfilling future. Past hurdles have created stror personal growth for you and now allow you to be propelled towards happiness.

December 19 – Last Quarter Moon in Virgo.

This Moon phase occurs at 04.57 UTC.

December 22 - December Solstice.

The 2019 December solstice occurs at 04:19 UTC. The South Pole of the earth tilts toward the Sun, which, having reached its most southern place in the sky, is directly over the Tropic of Capricorn at 23.44 degrees south latitude. This December solstice also marks the first day of winter (winter solstice) in the Northern Hemisphere.

December 21, 22 - Ursids Meteor Shower.

The Ursids meteor shower occurs each year from December 17 - 25. This meteor event peaks this year on the night of the 21st and morning of the 22nd.

December 26 - New Moon in Capricorn.

The Moon is on the same side of the Earth as the Sun and will not be visible in the night sky. This moon phase occurs at 05:15 UTC. This is an excellent time to view galaxies and stars because there is no moonlight visible.

Your energy is flowing a river of deep feelings during this time, heightening your intuition and emotional sensitivity. Cosmic forces are aligning which will likely help guide your path and allow you to manifest positive outcomes. It is a fortuitous time for you which is revitalizing to your energy.

December 26 - Annular Solar Eclipse.

An annular solar eclipse occurs because the Moon is too far away from the Earth to adequately hide the Sun. This results in a ring of light around the dark Moon. The Sun's corona is not visible during an annular eclipse.

There is radiant and inspired creative energy being sent to you during this annular solar eclipse. This effervescent energy shimmers through the essence of your imagination. Heightened awareness of creative energy is soon likely to result in emotions which are bewitching and radiant. You're being guided to explore your skills of storytelling, and allow your vivid imagination to effortlessly bring your creative endeavors to life.

*May the stars shine brightly on your world in 2019,
and beyond.*

About Crystal Sky

Crystal is passionate about the universe, helping others, and personal development. She writes yearly horoscopes books and astrologically minded diaries to celebrate the universal forces which affect us all. You can email Crystal at Crystal@OHoroscope.com or visit her site to learn more about her books. www.OHoroscope.com

When not writing about the stars, you can find Crystal under them, gazing up at the abundance that surrounds us all, with her pooch Henri by her side.

Notes:

Notes:

Made in the USA
Middletown, DE
18 December 2018